SERIES PREFACE

Food and food production have never had a higher profile, with food-related issues featuring in newspapers or on TV and radio almost every day. At the same time, educational opportunities related to food have never been greater. Food technology is taught in schools, as a subject in its own right, and there is a variety of food-related courses in colleges and universities - from food science and technology through nutrition and dietetics to catering and hospitality management.

Despite this attention, there is widespread misunderstanding of food - about what it is, about where it comes from, about how it is produced, and about its role in our lives. One reason for this, perhaps, is that the consumer has become distanced from the food production system as it has become much more sophisticated in response to the developing market for choice and convenience. Whilst other initiatives are addressing the issue of consumer awareness, feedback from the food industry itself and from the educational sector has highlighted the need for short focused overviews of specific aspects of food science and technology with an emphasis on industrial relevance.

The *Key Topics in Food Science and Technology* series of short books therefore sets out to describe some fundamentals of food and food production and, in addressing a specific topic, each issue emphasises the principles and illustrates their application through industrial examples. Although aimed primarily at food industry recruits and trainees, the series will also be of interest to those interested in a career in the food industry, food science and technology students, food technology teachers, trainee enforcement officers and, established personnel within industry seeking a broad overview of particular topics.

Leighton Jones
Series Editor

i

Campden & Chorleywood Food
Research Association Group

Key Topics in Food
Science and Technology – No. 4

Introduction to hygiene in food processing

Tim Hutton

Campden & Chorleywood Food Research Association Group comprises
Campden & Chorleywood Food Research Association
and its subsidiary companies
CCFRA Technology Ltd   CCFRA Group Services Ltd   Campden & Chorleywood Magyarország

© CCFRA 2001

Campden & Chorleywood Food
Research Association Group

Chipping Campden, Gloucestershire, GL55 6LD UK
Tel: +44 (0) 1386 842000   Fax: +44 (0) 1386 842100
www.campden.co.uk

© CCFRA 2001
ISBN: 0 905942 45 0

PREFACE TO THIS VOLUME

Food hygiene is increasingly important in the provision of safe and wholesome food. Whilst hygiene is often regarded as synonymous with cleanliness with an emphasis on microbial contaminants, there is, in fact, much more to it.

In its broadest sense, hygiene involves all measures taken to prevent contamination of food with any contaminant - be it microbiological, chemical or physical. Moreover, beyond the act of cleaning itself, hygiene is as much about the philosophy and practice of the whole approach. It impinges, for example, on the design of equipment (to ensure that cleaning can be as easy and as effective as possible), the layout of the premises (to encourage flows of materials and people so as not to encourage cross-contamination) and the development and management of cleaning regimes.

This short book presents an overview of hygiene in food processing. It emphasises that good hygienic practice is a combination of careful planning and effective execution. It describes potential contaminants and the routes by which they can enter foods, and then examines specific aspects of the food processing environment and their role in good hygienic practice - from premises, services and equipment through personnel hygiene and pest control to cleaning, disinfection and hygiene monitoring. In each case it describes the basic principles involved and then illustrates these with industrially relevant examples. Although it concentrates on hygiene in food processing areas, much of the information presented can be applied to domestic and catering food preparation.

Tim Hutton
CCFRA

ACKNOWLEDGEMENTS

In compiling this guide I am grateful to my colleagues Dr. Steven Walker and Dr. Leighton Jones, for helping to shape the document, and past and present members of the CCFRA Food Hygiene Department, most particularly Dr. John Holah, for guidance on specific technical details. Many of the examples used to illustrate specific points are drawn from other CCFRA publications and I am grateful to the authors of these (as cited) for providing the source material. Finally my thanks are also due to Rachel Prudden for the artwork and typesetting.

NOTE

All definitions, legislation, codes of practice and guidelines mentioned in this publication are included for the purposes of illustration only and relate to UK practice unless otherwise stated.

CONTENTS

1. INTRODUCTION – FOOD HYGIENE IN PERSPECTIVE

The are many facets to be considered in the implementation of a successful and all-encompassing hygiene programme in a food factory. It is not just about cleaning equipment and utensils, and ensuring that personnel do not contaminate the food in any way, it is also about making these aims easier to achieve. This includes correctly designing the factory itself, constructing it of the appropriate materials, ensuring that gas, water, electricity, waste disposal and other services are installed in a hygienic manner, and organising processing lines, work patterns and air flows to minimise the risk of contamination of product. As such it is about good practices as well as clean premises. Hygiene is relevant to all food production operations, but is especially vital in so-called high-risk and high-care activities (e.g. in chilled food production and in areas where the food may not be subsequently cooked before consumption). High-protein foods such as cooked meat, poultry and fish, dairy products and eggs, and cooked starchy foods such as rice are particularly vulnerable.

High care and high risk

Although good hygiene practices are relevant to all food production and processing areas, there are circumstances where they are particularly important. In high-care areas, such as a sandwich production facility, some of the ingredients are unprocessed (e.g. salad in the filling) and the product is not going to be subject to any further process which would reduce contamination levels. Thus, it is the combination of prevention of contamination and the assurance of good quality starting materials that are particularly important. In high-risk areas, such as areas producing cooked products that will be eaten cold, good hygiene practices are of paramount importance as they are the sole means of producing food free of microbial contamination.

Reference:

Holah, J. and Thorpe, R. (2000) The hygienic design of chilled foods plant. pp355-396 in Chilled Foods: a comprehensive guide (Eds. M. Stringer and C. Dennis)

"Food hygiene involves all measures to prevent contamination and thus to ensure the safety and wholesomeness of foods, and covers all stages after primary production (growing of the food), including offering for sale or supply to the consumer."

This paraphrase of the EU Food Hygiene Directive (Anon, 1993) illustrates that food hygiene is all-encompassing and covers microbial, chemical and physical contamination.

The food industry goes to great lengths to ensure that food, as sold and consumed, is free from contaminants that might make it unfit or unsafe to eat, or shorten its shelf-life to an unacceptable degree. There are two major strategies for achieving this. The first is to remove as many existing contaminants as is practically feasible, by using appropriate processing protocols. A good example of this is the removal of stones picked up during harvest of a vegetable or fruit. The second strategy is to prevent recontamination, through the adoption of good hygiene practices and the use of hygienically designed factories and equipment. It is the latter approach that is the focus of this Key Topic.

Although this book concentrates on hygiene in food productions areas, many of the topics discussed can be applied to harvesting and storage of raw materials, and especially to domestic and food preparation scenarios.

All processing needs to be carried out in a hygienic manner - that is, in a way that reduces to a minimum the chances of microbial, chemical or physical cross-contamination from the environment in general to the food, including from other food. There are many guidelines and codes of practice detailing how best to do this. General guidelines such as those produced by the Institute of Food Science and Technology (IFST, 1998) are widely used and accepted in the industry. There are also guidelines for specific food types, and for specific processes, such as that for heat-preserved foods produced by the Department of Health (DoH, 1994), and for matters relating to buildings, equipment and the environment. In simple terms, these guidelines detail all the relevant hygiene issues that have to be addressed in the manufacture of safe and palatable foods. This book discusses, in general terms, all of the hygiene issues that have to be addressed by food manufacturers.

1.1 Potential contaminants

Food contaminants fall into three basic categories: microbial, physical (e.g. foreign bodies such as glass or stones), and chemical. These generally reflect the nature of the food raw materials, which are mostly obtained from plants and animals farmed in an open environment. Both chemicals and micro-organisms of concern can occur naturally in the food raw material and all three types of hazard can potentially gain access to food during harvesting, processing and production. Good hygienic design and practice is about minimising the likelihood of such access occurring.

Microbial contaminants

Unlike chemical and physical contaminants, microbial contaminants can and will multiply over time, so that something that may start off as not a problem (i.e. a low level of contamination) may quickly become one. Some examples of microbial food contaminants are given in Table 1. Growth of micro-organisms will depend on a number of factors, such as temperature, humidity, availability of nutrients, and presence or absence of oxygen and inhibitory compounds such as preservatives. Different organisms require different conditions for optimal growth (e.g. some grow only in the absence of oxygen, others prefer either warm or cool conditions). Bacterial growth is by simple division of one cell into two (binary fission), and their number will increase exponentially under favourable conditions.

Pathogenic micro-organisms are the major food safety concern for the industry. As they are generally undetectable by the unaided human senses (i.e. they do not usually cause colour changes or produce off-flavours or taints in the food) and they are capable of rapid growth under favourable storage conditions, much time and effort is spent in controlling and/or eliminating them. The vast majority of outbreaks of food-related illness are due to pathogenic micro-organisms, rather than to chemical or physical contaminants. Even if micro-organisms in a food are destroyed by a subsequent cooking process, they may have previously produced toxins, so the prevention of contamination through good hygiene regimes remains vital.

As well as pathogenic micro-organisms, spoilage organisms can either be naturally present or gain access to food. Whilst not a food safety concern, increased levels of spoilage organisms will usually mean a reduction in the length of time that the food remains fit to eat. This can affect product quality and so also influence the consumer's perception of the product.

From a microbiological point of view, hygiene is about preventing contamination, preventing multiplication and destroying bacteria and other micro-organisms.

Table 1 - Examples of potential microbial contaminants and some typical sources

Listeria	General environment
Salmonella	Raw poultry
Staphylococcus	Human skin
Escherichia coli	Human/animal gut
Campylobacter	Human/animal gut
Cryptosporidium	Water
Fungal/mould spores	Air, condensation

Physical hazards

The variety of foreign body items that have been reportedly found in food over the years is considerable. Glass, stones, metal, poisonous berries, and insects can occur, and items as bizarre as whole rodents have been claimed. All of these can potentially gain access during the harvesting of raw materials, but most can also contaminate food during its processing (e.g. flies or glass falling onto the production line; metal flaking off a piece of machinery). Considerable effort goes into preventing contamination of foods with foreign bodies, and into the removal of those naturally or accidentally present in the raw material. Campbell (1995) provides a major overview of foreign body types and the methods used to prevent and detect their occurrence in foods.

Foreign body detection and removal methods

Depending on the nature of the food being processed and the equipment used for its processing, there are many techniques that can be used to detect and/or remove foreign bodies from food. Amongst these are:

- Metal detection systems
- X-ray systems
- Air separation systems
- Water separation systems
- Sieves and filters
- Magnets
- Electronic vision systems - based on shape, colour or opacity
- Human systems - manual sorting etc.

Reference:

Campbell, A.J. (1995) Guidelines for the prevention and control of foreign bodies in food. Guideline No. 5. Campden & Chorleywood Food Research Association.

Chemical contaminants

Food itself is made up entirely of chemicals. Other chemicals may be incorporated into food intentionally (as part of the process) or occasionally accidentally and may pose no risk at all. Others, which can pose a hazard at high enough levels, may unavoidably occur at very low levels. Many chemicals in food that do pose a food safety issue are not actually contaminants at all, but natural components of the food. Some are of microbiological origin, and while being highly undesirable, are 'naturally' associated with the food. Ironically, modern analytical techniques, which mean that we can now detect the presence of extremely low levels of contaminants and take preventative or remedial action, have focussed attention on the whole subject of potentially harmful chemicals in food. Some examples of potential chemical contaminants are given in Table 2. The industry takes great care to minimise the possibility of any potentially harmful chemical getting into food.

Although hygienic design and best practice are not the major tools for preventing many types of chemical contamination of foods, good protocols are required to ensure that lubricants, cleaning chemicals and disinfectants, for example, do not pose a problem. Taints from wall coverings or adhesives are also a potential concern.

Table 2 - Examples of potential chemical contaminants

Machinery lubricants

Cleaning detergents

Disinfectants

Floor coatings and resins

Paint from walls and ceiling

Pesticides (e.g. rodenticides)

Mycotoxins

1.2 Routes of contamination

Foods can become contaminated during growing and harvesting of the raw material (e.g. with soil and associated stones, micro-organisms), its storage and transport (e.g. with moulds or tainting chemicals), and its processing into the finished product (from processing equipment and the factory environment). Finished product may then be contaminated during subsequent storage and transport to shops, and during sale to and storage and preparation by the consumer.

The routes of contamination can be broadly divided into: people, pests, equipment and other surfaces, air and water (Holah, 1999). Many incidences may involve more than one vehicle - for example, transfer of microbial contamination from the hands to food via processing equipment, or aerosol droplets arising from people sneezing settling on the food directly. The main points to consider with these routes are discussed below.

Surfaces

Surfaces, especially food contact surfaces, are perhaps the most easily identifiable route of contamination to food products. The passage of food material over a surface leaves residual food debris and sometimes micro-organisms, which can, over time, multiply to sufficient numbers and result in a risk to the safety or quality of the food. The build-up of food debris, which may deteriorate when out of the main product flow, will also have an impact on product quality if it subsequently returns to the main product flow. Chemical contamination may also result from these contact surfaces if they are not adequately rinsed after cleaning and disinfection regimes. As well as surfaces over which the product flows, other contact items such as utensils and containers can be vectors of contamination.

Non-product contact surfaces, such as floors, walls, ceilings, overhead beams and equipment supports, are also important. As well as being reservoirs of microbial contamination, they can also be a source of physical and chemical contamination (e.g. from flaking plaster and the chemical residues within it). They need to be designed so that they can be effectively cleaned and so that they are stable to everyday wear and tear.

Water

Water is used in the food industry as an ingredient, as a production process aid, for cleaning, for fire safety and for domestic systems. Its use as an ingredient and as a processing aid can give rise to potential microbial or chemical contamination problems, and so it is important to use water of a high microbiological and chemical quality (i.e. of potable quality). Water used in handwashing facilities also poses a potential problem. Similarly, unwanted water, such as from steam or water vapour, condensation, leaking pipes or drains, or rainwater, can also be a vector for contamination, and pooled water is particularly hazardous as microbial levels can multiply rapidly under favourable conditions. The water used in cleaning and sanitising regimes also needs to be of adequate quality (see Holah, 1997; Dawson, 1998 and Dawson, 2000 for further information on the quality and use of water in the food industry).

Personnel

People are a large reservoir of micro-organisms. Many of these micro-organisms are harmless and incapable of surviving or multiplying in food, but gastrointestinal infections can be transferred to food (e.g. via aerosol droplets resulting from coughing near the process line). Pathogens on hands are also a potential source of contamination (Taylor and Holah, 2000). The whole subject of contamination of ready-to-eat foods by food preparation personnel has been the subject of a US Food and Drug Administration White Paper (Guzewich and Ross, 1999). People can also be a vector for contamination of food with objects, such as ear-rings, plasters and small personal belongings.

How many different species live in or on the human body and what is the actual total population of these guests?

This was a question put to New Scientist. In his reply, the Editor quoted some facts and figures from Theodore Rosebury's book 'Life on Man'. Amongst the facts quoted are that there may be around 80 distinguishable microbial species living in the mouth alone, and that the average number of bacteria excreted each day by an adult ranges from 100 billion to 100 trillion!

Micro-organisms inhabit every external surface of the body, including eyes, ears, nose and mouth. The hair is another major source of micro-organisms. It has been estimated that at least 200 different species are present in the human body. In addition to these, larger organisms can often be present; some of them are no more than irritants (e.g. lice), while others can cause a variety of illnesses.

For a description of some of the effects of these unpleasant guests, see New Scientist 30 Sep 2000 (inside back cover).

Pests

Pests such as birds, insects and rodents are potentially a major contamination problem, and particular care is taken to prevent their entry into food production areas. Floors and walls need to be designed so that they do not allow insects and other invertebrates the chance to live and breed, and buildings in general should be bird and rodent-proof. Preventing flying insects from entering the food processing area may not always be straight-forward, and electric 'Insectocutors' need to be suitably positioned to eradicate them.

Air

Air can be a significant medium for the transfer of contamination to food products (Brown, 1996). Micro-organisms will be present, often in aerosols, and the air is likely to be the main route for contamination with 'light' foreign bodies such as dust, straw-type debris, and insects. Chemical taints can enter the production area if a chemical processing plant is located nearby, or if there is a significant fire in the vicinity.

1.3 Preventing contamination - HACCP and hygiene in partnership

The internationally recognised philosophy used to help ensure the production of safe foods is HACCP (Hazard Analysis and Critical Control Points). EC hygiene directives state that food production processes must be evaluated and controlled using systems based on hazard analysis. In the UK, HACCP-based systems are now being introduced in all parts of the food supply chain, from agricultural production, through processing and manufacturing, to retail sale. However, their use in assuring that appropriate hygiene measures are taken in food processing areas arguably remains their most important application.

Many books describe the philosophy of HACCP - see Leaper (1997) and Mortimore and Wallace (1998) for examples. One of the main advantages of HACCP (which was originally devised by the Pillsbury Company to ensure the safety of food on board manned space missions) is that the need for end-product testing is reduced to a minimum and is replaced by systematic and targeted preventative measures. For example, it is not necessary to do exhaustive microbiological testing of product if the HACCP study indicates that microbiological levels are being properly controlled (although some such testing may be required, together with specific measures for monitoring the effectiveness of the controls). This frees resources to enable targeted testing which can be more informative.

practice, good hygiene practices are one of the major control measures used to support and fulfil a HACCP study.

The HACCP approach is based on seven internationally recognized simple principles:

1) Conduct a hazard analysis: prepare a flow diagram of the steps in the process; identify and list the hazards associated with the process and specify how they are going to be controlled.

2) Determine the critical control points (CCPs), i.e. those stages at which hazard control is essential for the production of a safe end-product.

3) Establish critical limits for each hazard at each CCP, i.e. the levels for each individual hazard that must not be exceeded if a safe product is going to be achieved. This may, for example, be a maximum storage temperature, or a maximum limit for a particular micro-organism, or a minimum salt level in the product.

4) Set up a system to monitor control of each CCP by scheduled testing and observations, to ensure that the hazard remains within critical limits.

5) Establish what corrective action needs to be taken if monitoring indicates that a particular CCP is not under control or is moving out of control, i.e. is going beyond critical limits - this means stopping something going wrong before it happens, if at all possible.

6) Set up procedures to make sure that the overall HACCP plan is working as desired; this may include some end-product testing and a regular review of the system.

7) Establish thorough documentation of the system, process and procedures, and of all measurements taken relating to the monitoring of the process.

Software programmes (such as CCFRA's *HACCP Documentation Software* and *safefood Process Design System*) are available to help companies formulate, monitor, control and record their HACCP systems.

HACCP and hygiene - example

The hygiene procedures that might need to be taken to support part of a HACCP plan will vary depending on the nature of the product and the way in which it is being processed. Indeed, two factories producing nearly identical products may have some significantly different sections of their HACCP plans, due perhaps to the physical nature or positioning of the factory. A few typical examples are given below, for a chilled food production line:

Hazards	Hygiene Controls
Foreign bodies entering product	Pest exclusion systems Insectocutors Maintenance of wall and ceiling finishes Protection of overhead lighting
Presence of microbial pathogens	Adequate cleaning of production line Adequate air filtering system Adequate cleaning of utensils and equipment Hand wash on entry to production area

References:

Campbell, A.J. (1995) Guidelines for the prevention and control of foreign bodies in food. Guideline No. 5. Campden & Chorleywood Food Research Association.

Leaper, S. (1997) HACCP: A practical guide. Technical Manual No. 38. 2nd Edition. Campden & Chorleywood Food Research Association

Other examples of factors which will support a HACCP system for the prevention of contamination are to have adequate storage space available to cope with fluctuation in demand (cramped conditions may hinder cleaning and allow contamination to go un-noticed), and to have an effective system of stock rotation - old stock can deteriorate and contaminate fresh stock.

1.4 Hygiene legislation

In addition to the commercial imperative for supplying consumers with safe food, there has been much EU-wide legislation that requires companies to comply with hygienic standards and practices. In the UK this has been enacted via the Food Safety (General Food Hygiene) Regulations, and individual regulations covering dairy products, egg products, fish and shellfish products, and fresh meat, minced meat, poultry meat, wild game and meat products.

These regulations are extensive in their requirements and in many cases include prescribed maximum levels for specified micro-organisms (e.g. *Listeria*, *Salmonella* and coliforms). However, there are some inconsistencies between the general hygiene legislation and some of the individual requirements (e.g. regarding materials that may be used in the processing area). At the time of writing, EU legislation is being proposed that will draw all of the legislation together and result in the different food products being subject to broadly the same requirements. The industry is, by nature, very cautious over the materials and equipment it uses, and the new legislation, when it is passed, is unlikely to have a major effect on the industry, and in most cases will merely put into statute the good practices already in operation.

The legislation and recommended practices in place are monitored by enforcement officers (typically Environmental Health Officers in the UK). Their inspection regimes will normally involve assessment of:

- temperature controls at all stages of product handling/processing
- cleaning regimes - schedules and effectiveness
- personnel hygiene (including procedures, facilities, training and attitude)
- preventative controls - e.g. pest control, stock rotation, general awareness of staff
- infrastructure - such as factory layout, design of specific areas, lighting, ventilation, and washing facilities.

2. PREMISES AND SERVICES

In order for food to be produced hygienically, the building in which it is processed and the facilities and services used must be of a suitable standard. The building itself must also be suitably located - that is, not in areas that are prone to flooding or where there is a significant problem with air pollution. Many foods (especially those with a high fat content) may be susceptible to tainting, and although precautions can be taken to minimise the amount of external atmosphere entering the production area, locations where smoke or fumes from chemical factories are a problem should be avoided.

It is also important to design the interior of the building correctly, in terms of equipment lay-out. The following sections detail the importance of air and personnel movements, and of preventing product build-up on processing lines. If the processing line itself is incorrectly laid out or inappropriately placed, no amount of rules on personnel activities, or air filtration systems and cleaning regimes will enable adequate overall hygiene standards to be attained. For example, processing lines should not be positioned so that the opening of doors results in direct draughts over a high-risk area (e.g. chilled food preparation area), and operatives should not have to pass through high-risk areas while carrying out their normal duties in low-risk areas.

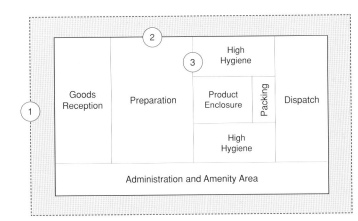

Figure 1 - Schematic layout of a factory site showing 'barriers' against contamination.
(1) Perimeter fence; (2) Main factory buildings; (3) Walls of high-care area.

2.1 Production areas (walls, floors and ceilings)

The installation of state-of-the-art hygienically designed equipment and use of the latest tried and tested cleaning regimes will be of no benefit if the walls and floors are badly designed and cannot be adequately cleaned, or if they are prone to flaking, disintegration or condensation. The basic considerations for floors, walls and ceilings are discussed below.

Floors

The floor in a food factory forms the basis of the entire processing operation, and a failure in the floor often results in lengthy disruptions of production and financial loss while repairs are carried out (Timperley, 1993). Thus, both its physical durability and hygienic qualities have to be considered. The overall design of the floor must be such that it can be effectively cleaned and disinfected, is safe in use (e.g. anti-slip) and that it is stable under these cleaning regimes and to normal processing activities (i.e. does not begin to disintegrate, which may result in microbial or physical contamination of the food being processed). A section of a typical floor is shown in Figure 2.

As part of the design of floors, allowance has to be made for adequate drainage of water - that is, the physical shape of the floor should allow water to easily drain away. A slope (or 'fall') of 1 in 60 is normally adequate; 1 in 40 may be required for floors that are habitually very wet, whilst 1 in 80 may be sufficient for normally dry tiled floors. There are many designs of drainage falls, which are described by Timperley (1993); outlets should preferably be of stainless steel for ease of cleaning.

The structural floor slab (i.e. the base on which the top layer of flooring will sit) should be capable of withstanding all structural, thermal and mechanical stresses and loads which will occur during service, as a failure will compromise the hygienic properties of the top-layer flooring. In particular, allowances should be made for expansion, contraction and cracking, and where appropriate for problems arising from hydrostatic pressure and rising damp. This can, under certain circumstances, cause the adhesion between the floor slab and flooring to fail. In general, the floor slab should be free from contamination, dry and finished with a strong, even surface.

Figure 2 - Typical layers in a concrete ground floor

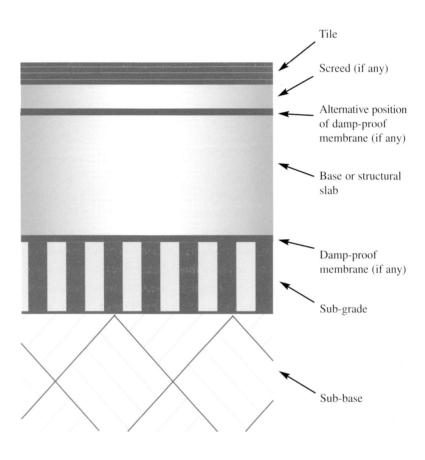

Tile

Screed (if any)

Alternative position
of damp-proof
membrane (if any)

Base or structural
slab

Damp-proof
membrane (if any)

Sub-grade

Sub-base

This figure shows a cross section of a typical tiled, concrete factory ground floor, illustrating the various layers necessary to provide the required strength, stability and other properties (e.g. damp proofing).

All wet- or corrosion-resistant floorings need to be laid on a waterproof and acid-resistant membrane. This is particularly important in the design of suspended floors, where deflection due to heavy moving loads may cause cracks or fissures through which corrosive liquids (or water during cleaning operations) might pass to damage the structural concrete. Some of the main requirements of the membranes are that they should be:

- Resistant and impermeable to specified liquids (depending on factory use)
- Continuous
- Strong enough to support imposed loads and resist damage during flooring repairs
- Capable of flexing
- Extended up the walls to a height above the normal spillage level
- Carried over plinths or kerbs, below drainage channels and into drains

The flooring material itself can be made of a number of different substances. Although concrete is resistant to chemical attack from alkalis, mineral oils and many salts, it is attacked by acids, vegetable and animal oils, sugar solutions and some salts. It is also porous and tends to crumble under impact or when abraded. As such, it is not generally considered to be suitable as a flooring material for most food processing areas. However, it can be improved by various means so that it can be used in some food storage and access areas.

Ceramic tiles, made from clay, are commonly used as flooring materials. Fully vitrified tiles are most suitable for their hygienic properties, being resistant to bacterial ingress and easy to clean. The surfaces may be smooth, studded or incorporate silicon carbide granules to further enhance slip resistance. However, increased slip resistance usually means an increased difficulty in cleaning, and therefore different tile surfaces may be suitable for different parts of the factory. The tiles need to be laid properly, or else the intrinsic hygienic qualities of the tiles will be negated. They must be solidly bedded with no voids beneath; the joints between the tiles should be between 3 and 10 mm (depending on the tile type and bedding system), and should be grouted as soon as possible so as to avoid contamination. The joints should be finished flush with the surface of the tiles.

Resin-based seamless floorings also allow high standards of hygienic conditions to be achieved. Various resin-based systems are suitable - epoxy, polyurethane, polyester and methacrylate - and can be laid to different thicknesses, depending on the exact requirements of the factory area. These compounds can impart taints to food if laid whilst food production is continuing, and so appropriate precautions must be taken, and taint tests should be carried out.

Walls

Like floors, the physical construction of walls, both external and internal, is important in maintaining the integrity of the internal finish - the part of the wall that faces onto the food processing area. These are dealt with in detail in Timperley (1994) and a typical factory wall is depicted in cross-section in Figure 3. The material of which the walls are constructed (the background) are not usually suitable for direct application of a coating and most require a render and/or plaster finish to cover surface imperfections and unevenness. This should provide a hygienic, crevice-free surface with suitable keying properties for the final finish to be applied. The type of background used (e.g. brick, block or concrete) will influence the choice of render or plaster used.

The coating applied as the top layer must result in a finish that is smooth, easy to clean, durable and impermeable. Material used should also be non-toxic. Liquid paint-based systems comprise a primer, one or more undercoats and one or more finishing coats. The finishing coats may be emulsion paints, oil-based, epoxy or polyurethane paints, or chlorinated or acrylated rubber paints. In areas where high levels of humidity or condensation occur regularly, it may be necessary to apply a fungicidal paint system to control the growth of moulds. Some paint systems rely on leaching of chemicals from within the paint to control mould growth; these types of paint are not generally considered suitable for use in food processing areas because of the potential contamination and taint hazard.

Reinforced liquid coatings, based on glass fibres mixed with an epoxy resin, can be used to provide a smooth finish which is easy to clean, and also gives good resistance to many chemicals, impact damage, and abrasion, all of which are good hygienic features. However, taint problems can potentially arise during their application.

Ceramic wall tiles are particularly suitable for areas that need to be frequently washed down, and where abrasion and/or heat resistance is required. As with floor tiles, correct adhesion to the wall is essential, as is complete grouting.

Although it is preferable to form the internal finish as an integral part of the wall structure, various cladding systems of polypropylene, polyvinyl chloride or stainless steel can be used in some circumstances. However, great care has to be taken to prevent mould growth or infestation with pests such as spiders and insects, in areas where the cladding is not flush with the background wall.

The overall shape of the wall is also important. The presence of ledges and similar features (e.g. around windows) can result in a significant hazard as regards accumulation of debris, and this has to be considered at the design stage.

Covings

Having installed hygienically suitable floors and walls, it is important that floor-to-wall, wall-to-wall and wall-to-ceiling joints are hygienically constructed. Covings should provide an easily cleaned surface at wall, floor and ceiling junctions. A 50mm radius curve or a 50 x 50mm deep chamfer is generally considered to be large enough to enable easy cleaning (although extra consideration will have to be made to prevent damage from moving traffic such as trolleys and fork-lift trucks).

In floor-to-wall junctions, a 50mm radius resin cove or a coved tile can be used, depending on the nature of the flooring material (tiles tend to be 30 mm in radius). The upper join of this is terminated by a galvanised or stainless steel stop bead secured to the wall, with the wall render finishing above this bead. Silicone sealant is used between the tile or resin and the stop bead to allow for thermal or other movement of the wall and flooring.

Figure 3 - Section of a typical factory wall end and its joint with flooring

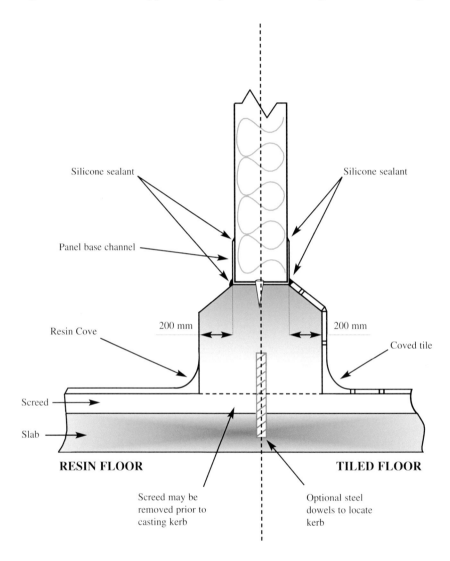

Silicone sealant

Silicone sealant

Panel base channel

Resin Cove

200 mm

200 mm

Coved tile

Screed

Slab

RESIN FLOOR

TILED FLOOR

Screed may be
removed prior to
casting kerb

Optional steel
dowels to locate
kerb

The join between a wall and the floor is best designed with the end-use of the area in mind. The figure here shows the examples of resin and tile covered floors adjoining a wall which is protected by kerbing because it is exposed to trolley and/or fork-lift traffic.

Ceilings

The main considerations for ceilings from a hygiene point of view is to ensure that they do not become a harbour for insects and other pests, or for microbial growth, and particularly that they are not susceptible to condensation, flaking or disintegration. Clearly small fragments of debris falling from the ceiling could pose a significant hazard to the production line, and small fragments could travel a significant distance laterally (i.e. not drop straight down). Within these constraints there are several options available for a hygienic ceiling, and the nature of the existing roof (if the building is being refurbished) and location of services (gas, water, air, electricity etc) are likely to influence the final decision.

2.2 Services - general

Having constructed floors, walls and ceilings hygienically, it is important that the positioning of pipes and ancillary services does not compromise the overall design. Service pipes should be routed outside the process area and pass through walls local to their point of usage, wherever possible. In processing areas, they are usually constructed of stainless or galvanised steel or PVC, which are relatively easy to clean. Overhead pipes should not pass over open vessels or production lines, because of the risk of dripping condensation, leaks, and flaking paint, lagging or dust. Painted steel in general should be avoided because of the risk of flaking. They also need to be positioned at least 50 mm away from floors and walls so that they can be adequately inspected, cleaned, maintained and repaired.

Non-potable water (e.g. for steam production, refrigeration or fire control) needs to be readily identified and routed away from processing areas, and must have no connection with the water used for washing and cooling food products. Cables need to be enclosed in structural conduits which are accessible for cleaning, pest control and maintenance.

Good lighting is essential in the processing area so that operatives can carry out monitoring and control work effectively, and should be of at least 500 lux. It is also vital for maintenance and cleaning staff to be able to do their jobs properly.

Lighting may need to be positioned directly over processing lines which, as it involves the use of glass, presents a serious risk of glass contamination of the processing line unless adequate precautions are taken. Potential problems can be reduced by ensuring that safety shields/meshes are used to prevent glass from falling on the line, and by putting procedures in place to stop the process line and remove all debris, should a breakage occur. Wherever possible, glass should be avoided in food handling areas.

2.3 Air systems

Air can be a major vector for contamination of the food processing environment, as outlined in section 1.2, and there has been much interest recently in air flow in food processing areas, especially high-care areas. Here microbial contamination of products is a major hazard (usually because the product is not going to be subsequently cooked or preserved in some way) and this has significant implications for hygienic food production. Brown (1996) discusses air control systems and their monitoring and maintenance in great detail.

Openings in the walls around the process area should be kept to a minimum in order to limit the risk of pest access and airborne contamination. For the same reason, natural ventilation should be avoided, as it cannot be controlled. Combined air supply and extract systems allow a balanced and controlled air flow. These will allow a positive air pressure to be maintained in the production area (of at least 10-15 Pascals), and will incorporate suitable air filtration mechanisms to remove most airborne particles and micro-organisms from the incoming air. They will also allow removal from the processing area of hot or stale air, which may be relatively humid and contain higher levels of dust particles. It is very important that the chosen system be regularly cleaned and maintained or there is a risk that it will blow more contamination into the processing area than it removes.

Control of airborne microbial contamination in high-care areas

In a joint project between CCFRA and Silsoe Research Institute, the fate of airborne micro-organisms was investigated in food environments. Computational fluid dynamics (CFD) were used to predict the movement of airborne particles, and these predictions were compared with actual environmental measurements. CFD tracking showed particle movement from hatches and doors. Pressure differentials allowed particles to be drawn from 'low-care' areas to the 'high-care' area, giving rise to a potential hygiene problem. Relating this to actual microbial counts demonstrated that airborne organisms which entered the high-care area would disperse and potentially land on and contaminate exposed product. Changing the position of hatches and doorways and the location of the ventilation inlets could alleviate this problem.

Reference:

Burfoot, D. *et al.* (2001) Best practice guidelines on air flows in high-care and high risk areas. Silsoe Research Institute

Airflow within the factory is also very important. Generally, this should be from clean or high-risk areas to dirty or low-risk areas. Holah *et al.* (1995) found that microbial counts in 60-litre air samples varied between 1 and 500, depending on the activity in the area. Recent work (Burfoot *et al.* 2001) has investigated the effects of the opening of doors in different parts of the processing area on airflow dynamics. Brown and Hall (1999) have also tried to quantify the risks of airborne contamination of food in processing areas and the factors that influence it. A significant finding was that surface charge enhanced aerosol deposition and this has relevance in the development of processing procedures and equipment.

Restricted airflow caused spoilage

Genetic fingerprinting techniques have illustrated how important factory lay-out can be, and how changes can have unforeseen effects that compromise product quality or safety. A food company was having problems with product spoilage, and conventional microbiological analysis had implicated pseudomonads, but could not pinpoint the source. Using fingerprinting technique, the strain isolated from the spoiled food was matched exactly with that found in condensation on processing equipment. Further investigation revealed that the condensation had arisen because of changes in plant layout which had reduced airflow. Having identified the cause, remedial action was taken to increase airflow in relevant areas and so eliminate the problem.

2.4 Water systems

Water is used both as an ingredient and as a processing aid in food manufacture and is thus a significant potential source of microbiological and chemical contamination. In both cases it is a legal requirement that it is of high quality. There are two good examples where the use of water as a processing aid has significant implications from a food hygiene point of view; these are in the cooling of cans and other heat-treated containers, and in the washing of fresh produce.

At the end of a pasteurisation or sterilisation process, canned foods are normally cooled as rapidly as possible in cold water. This is to prevent the product from being over-cooked, and also to prevent the germination of spores of any thermophilic spoilage micro-organisms that might have survived the heat treatment process (Thorpe and Everton, 1968). During this cooling process, there is the potential for micro-organisms in the water to enter the can through the seal between the body of the can and the lid. For this reason the cans must not be handled while still hot and wet, and the water used must be of high microbiological quality. The cause of an infamous typhoid food poisoning outbreak in 1964 in Aberdeen, linked with corned beef, was traced back to post-process contamination. The cans had been cooled in the open air with water from the local river, downstream from a military fort where a typhoid outbreak had occurred! There are anecdotal reports of people still not buying corned beef because of this incident. In order to ensure that the bacterial count in the water used is low, it is often chlorinated before use; this has proved to be a very effective way of ensuring that water quality is satisfactory, and post-process contamination of cans is now a very rare event.

Washing of fresh produce is performed to remove microbial, chemical and physical contaminants from the products that have gained access during the growing, harvesting and storage/transport of the food. It is important to ensure that additional contamination is not introduced during this process. A review of industry practice in the UK food industry by Seymour (1999) revealed that over three quarters used chlorine as a washing sanitiser; the levels of chlorine varied enormously, depending on the nature of the product being washed (up to 600ppm chlorine), and bacterial levels on the produce were reduced by approximately 100-fold.

Recent work has looked at the use of chlorine dioxide and bromine as alternatives to chlorine for the treatment of food industry process waters (Holah, 1997). Although chlorine has many advantages, it is not effective in alkaline conditions and it can react with nitrogenous and other organic materials, resulting in a loss of activity and sometimes the formation of environmentally unacceptable compounds. This might be a particular problem in the washing of 'very dirty' fresh produce. Antiseptic taint compounds can also be formed, which could be transferred to the product. However, chlorine dioxide and bromine also have their disadvantages, and it is likely that each agent will have applications where it is most suitable.

3. HYGIENIC DESIGN OF EQUIPMENT

Having constructed buildings and installed services that provide good hygienic conditions, it is important that the food processing equipment in the factory is also designed and installed to good hygiene standards. The overall objective is that the equipment and machinery used should minimise the level of contamination that is likely to occur, and that it should be easy to clean.

3.1 General considerations

All food processing equipment in the EC must comply with the 'machinery directive' (98/37/EC), which states that machinery intended for the preparation and processing of foods must be designed and constructed so as to avoid health risks. The directive also lists seven hygiene rules that must be observed; these are broadly similar to those cited below. A series of documents published by the European Hygienic Equipment Design Group (EHEDG) gives recommendations for a wide range of specific equipment design features.

Design of equipment to minimise contaminant build-up includes not only how individual pieces are constructed, but also how they all fit together on the process line and how the line is laid out in the factory. However, during food processing, build-up of debris and soil is inevitable as, potentially, is microbial build-up in this debris. The contamination of high-quality food with either the physical debris or the associated micro-organisms is highly undesirable, and equipment design must also make it as easy as possible to remove this.

The seven basic principles of hygienic design (based on Jowett, 1980 and CFDRA, 1982) are:

♦ All surfaces in contact with food should be inert to the food under the conditions of use and must not migrate to, or be absorbed by, the food.

- All surfaces in contact with food should be smooth and non-porous so that tiny particles of food, bacteria or other contaminants are not caught in microscopic surface crevices and difficult to dislodge, thus becoming a potential source of contamination

- All surfaces in contact with the food should be visible for inspection, or the equipment must be readily disassembled for inspection, or it should be demonstrated that routine cleaning procedures eliminate the possibility of contamination from bacteria or other organisms.

- All surfaces in contact with food should be readily accessible for manual cleaning, or if clean-in-place techniques are used, it should be demonstrated that the results achieved without disassembly are the equivalent of those obtained with disassembly and manual cleaning

- All interior surfaces in contact with food should be arranged so that the equipment is self-emptying or self-draining

- Equipment should be designed so as to protect the contents from external contamination

- The exterior or non-product contact surfaces should be arranged to prevent harbouring of soils, bacteria and pests in and on the equipment itself as well as in its contact with other equipment, floors, walls or hanging supports

Specific general rules are to avoid dead spaces and other conditions which trap food and are difficult to clean, and to ensure that the equipment itself does not result in product contamination (e.g. through lagging breaking up or insufficiently secured nuts and bolts). Regarding the latter consideration, the use of wood is strongly discouraged in most food processing applications, as wooden surfaces are liable to splinter and contaminate the product; they are also very difficult to clean and disinfect thoroughly. Similarly, as mentioned in the services section, the use of glass should be avoided wherever possible, as glass fragments pose a major hazard in terms of product safety.

If paints and other non-product-contact surface treatments are required (e.g. to protect the joint areas between machine components), this should be done adequately to prevent the occurrence of corrosion, but should also not pose a chemical contamination problem.

Situations where specific problems may arise, and where particular care needs to be taken, are in the installation of guard machinery and noise suppression equipment, both of which may conflict with the general hygiene requirements. For example, guard machinery may be designed to protect hands but may be difficult to clean.

3.2 Design features for equipment

Each piece of equipment will have its own inherent design problems that need to be addressed. These will vary enormously, depending on the functions of the equipment. The variety of equipment used in the food industry is considerable, ranging from cutting, slicing, grinding and pressing machines, through agglomerators, blenders, moulders and spray dryers, to final product handling machines. The Food Trades Directory (Hemming Information Services Ltd, London) lists over 1000 categories of equipment and a similar number of UK suppliers of such equipment. The examples described below give a broad picture of the hygiene implications that have to be considered in the design of particular pieces of food processing equipment. While the details vary from case to case, the general principle will be to minimise or eliminate opportunities for debris to accumulate and to make cleaning and maintenance as easy as possible.

- ◆ Materials of construction. These need to be strong enough for their purpose over a wide temperature range, and for the lifetime of the equipment. They should be resistant to corrosion and abrasion, not taint the product, and not pass their constituents to the food in any detrimental way. Many types of stainless steel meet these basic requirements; those containing molybdenum are used where extra corrosion resistance is required, but steels containing up to 18% chromium or 8-10% nickel are also used. Aluminium is resistant to corrosion by many foods, and is light, easy to machine, and easy to cast into complex shapes. However, it is susceptible to corrosion by both sodium hydroxide and sodium hypochlorite, which form the basis of many detergents and disinfectants, respectively, in the food industry.

♦ Surface finish. Product contact surfaces must be smooth enough to be easily cleaned. Over time and use, the surface will become abraded and more difficult to clean. Plastics are more easily abraded than metals and this may adversely affect their cleanability, as the rougher the surface, the more likely it is to harbour product soil and the more difficult it will be to clean. Also, product soil will be easier to observe on shinier surfaces.

♦ Joints. Permanent joints should preferably be made by welding or continuous bonding so as to reduce projections, edges and recesses to a minimum. The joints must be smooth and have neither ridges nor crevices which could harbour organic materials. The welds need to be ground and polished to a standard of finish equal to that of the surrounding material. Joints which can be taken apart must be free of crevices and have a smooth, continuous surface on the product side. They need to be sealed against the ingress of product, micro-organisms and cleaning fluids by means of a gasket.

♦ Nuts, bolts, screws and rivets. Wherever possible, exposed threads, bolts and rivets should be avoided in product contact areas. They will cause product to accumulate and they are particularly difficult to clean. There are several types of hygienic fasteners (see Figure 4 for an example).

♦ Drainage. All pipelines and equipment surfaces should be self-draining. This will help to prevent microbial growth in the residual liquid, and aid in the removal of cleaning fluids which might otherwise contaminate the product.

♦ Internal angles and corners. As with covings for floors, walls and ceilings, these should be suitably radiused, to aid cleaning.

Figure 4 - Examples of an hygienic fastener using a sealing washer

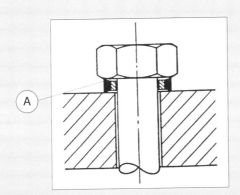

Although there are no difficult-to-clean slots or sockets in the hexagon head of a screw or bolt, there is a metal/metal joint which must be sealed if the ingress of micro-organisms is to be prevented. Sealing can be achieved by the use of a metal-backed rubber washer (A). The washer comprises a metal ring around which a wedge-shaped rubber ring is bonded. The head of the hexagon screw is shown just making contact with the outer edge of the rubber. The screw can be fully tightened, but the inner metal ring prevents over-compression of the rubber and allows the required tightening torque to be applied.

◆ Dead spaces. Dead spaces (Figure 5) or 'dead legs' will allow product to accumulate during production runs, permitting the growth of micro-organisms, and resulting in the slow or intermittent release of micro-organisms or degraded product into the product stream over time. Cleaning fluids will not be able to effectively clean these areas, and may subsequently be themselves difficult to remove, resulting in product contamination.

◆ Bearings. Bearings should, wherever possible, be mounted outside of the product area. Bearing lubricants should be prevented from contaminating the product, and similarly product should be prevented from gaining access to the bearings and possibly causing them to fail.

◆ Instrument Controls. Control panels that are frequently touched by food handlers in the operation of the process line should be easily cleanable.

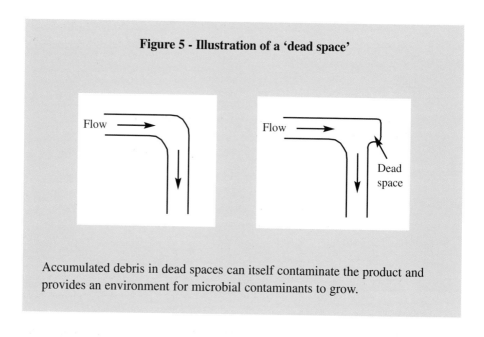

Figure 5 - Illustration of a 'dead space'

Accumulated debris in dead spaces can itself contaminate the product and provides an environment for microbial contaminants to grow.

3.3 Specific examples of equipment design

3.3.1 Processing line equipment

When the purchase of large or expensive items of food processing equipment is being considered, factors relating to hygienic design generally receive detailed attention as part of the overall assessment for suitability, as they will affect the operating efficiency, cost and lifespan of the piece of equipment. However, there is a danger that product transfer systems may be missed out of this assessment, as they are generally small and relatively inexpensive items, and are often installed on a temporary basis. However, good hygienic design and/or layout of conveyer belts, hoppers, chutes and other similar equipment is of fundamental importance in reducing the risk of product contamination to a minimum. An example looking at fruit and vegetable product transfer systems is given in CFDRA (1983) and illustrated in Figure 6. In addition to the general points of equipment design mentioned in section 3, the following points specific to product transfer were noted as potential problems:

- The incorrect location of adjoining equipment, resulting in inefficient transfer of product from one unit to the next. This could result in product wastage, and importantly from a hygiene point of view, build-up of debris around the main processing area.

- Design faults which allow the product to lodge out of the main flow. This is a significant problem, as this trapped product is likely to deteriorate and allow microbial growth, and may subsequently be reincorporated into the main product flow.

- The use of unsuitable fastenings which may work loose and cause damage to other equipment (and knock-on effects on other issues of hygiene) or even become incorporated into the product flow.

- Conveyor belts running at the wrong speed, which might result in excessive depth of product, and subsequent spillage.

Variations on the above points could potentially occur at any point in the production line. Specific areas such as catwalks, inspection tables, and product elevators have their own particular problems which have to be addressed.

Design, installation and maintenance

Good design must ensure the efficient functioning, safe operation and cost-effectiveness during the designed working life of the equipment, together with materials and construction which permit efficient and hygienic operation, maintenance and cleaning.

Care must be taken during the layout, planning and installation to ensure that unhygienic conditions do not arise. Engineering maintenance, whether preventative or breakdown, needs to be done in a way which results in hygienic conditions being retained.

CFDRA (1982) The principles of design for hygienic food processing machinery. Technical Memorandum 289. Campden & Chorleywood Food Research Association.

**Figure 6 - Illustration of some hygienic design features of a
fruit/vegetable conveyer system**

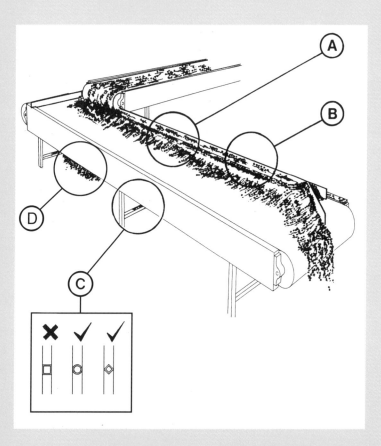

A Product   - Uneven distribution of product, arising from the
unsatisfactory discharge from the first conveyor,
results in a ridge of product along near side of the
inspection belt. This makes efficient inspection
impracticable.

B Debris - Product surges from the first conveyor cause "waves" of product to pass down the inspection belt. This in turn causes product to be pushed high up the side of the guide, leaving a "tide line" out of the main product flow.

C Frame-member - Flat horizontal support members provide surfaces on which debris can lodge. These should be replaced by tubular section material or square section members turned through 45° to provide sloping surfaces.

D Unsatisfactory discharge - Feed from the first conveyor results in only about $1/3$ width of second conveyor being used. As product builds up on the second conveyor, it falls to the floor and collects on the horizontal surfaces of the frames.

3.3.2 Liquid handling equipment

Most food processing lines involve the use of liquids at some stage in the process. The hygienic construction of pipelines, stirrers, valves and pumps present specific problems to the food industry (for full details see Timperley, 1997). Liquid is particularly prone to pooling in dead-ends, especially those below the level of the main flow of liquid.

As mentioned above for other food-contact surfaces, the surface finish and non-corrosivity of liquid handling systems are major factors in their design and construction. However, there are certain applications, particularly when highly acidic products containing chlorides are handled, when plastics are superior to stainless steel. The most widely used plastic materials for rigid pipes are polyvinylchloride (PVC), acrylonitrile butadiene systems, and polypropylene. Plastic pipes are lighter and cheaper than stainless steel, but the maximum temperature at which they can be used is much lower (below 100°C); they also need a greater degree of support to prevent sagging, especially at higher temperatures - sagging would cause liquid to pool, and thus pose a hygiene hazard (Figure 7). Flexible pipes and hoses can be made of PVC, ethylene vinyl acetate, low density polyethylene, nylon, polytetrafluoroethylene (PTFE) or reinforced natural or synthetic rubber. The latter are used mainly in the brewing and dairy industries for emptying or filling road tankers.

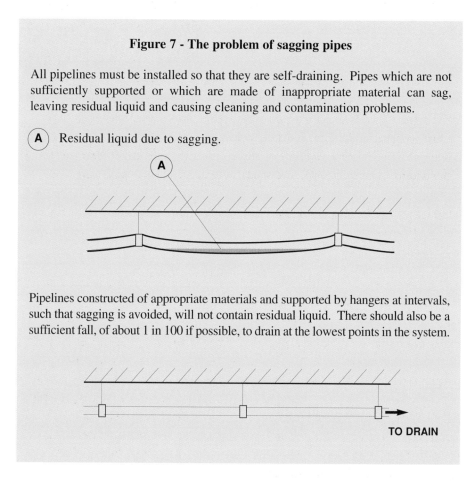

Figure 7 - The problem of sagging pipes

All pipelines must be installed so that they are self-draining. Pipes which are not sufficiently supported or which are made of inappropriate material can sag, leaving residual liquid and causing cleaning and contamination problems.

(**A**) Residual liquid due to sagging.

Pipelines constructed of appropriate materials and supported by hangers at intervals, such that sagging is avoided, will not contain residual liquid. There should also be a sufficient fall, of about 1 in 100 if possible, to drain at the lowest points in the system.

TO DRAIN

The best way of connecting stainless steel pipes is orbital welding. This is an automated process and if machinery is set up correctly and the ends of the pipes are properly prepared, consistent welds of good quality are produced which do not require polishing. If this is not possible, there are a variety of couplings that can be used, depending on the nature (especially viscosity) of the material to be carried.

Whatever type of coupling is used, it should allow efficient cleaning of the pipes, and not result in product or cleaning fluid being trapped in crevices or protrusions.

A variety of valves are used for controlling the flow of liquids, for shut-off, diversion, pressure and flow regulation, pressure relief and non-return. The valves have to satisfy various hygiene requirements. Materials used for gaskets, seals or soft seatings must be compatible with the fluids to be handled, including detergents and disinfectants; they must also be capable of withstanding the associated temperatures. As most valves are incorporated into systems which are cleaned in-place, internal surface finish is important, and this should be similar to that required for pipes and couplings. The internal geometry of the valve should ensure that it is cleanable in-place, self-draining and gives a smooth uninterrupted flow; this is especially important if the product is of high viscosity or contains suspended solids, as these are likely to pose more of a cleaning problem. Attention must also be paid to the installation of valves, to ensure that they are self-draining and do not form dead legs, especially when they are grouped together. Leakage detectors need to be incorporated, where appropriate, to indicate failure of diaphragms, membranes or seals.

A wide range of pumps, stirrers and agitators are used in liquid handling systems. With pumps, particular attention needs to be paid to the avoidance of crevices and 'dead' spaces, and to ensuring that the finish is adequate for cleaning and that the casing can be drained. With stirrers and agitators, potential problem areas are shaft sealing, blade attachment, shaft couplings, mounting arrangements and foot bearings. In addition, the parts of the stirrer or agitator that are external to the tank or vessel should be designed and constructed to minimise the accumulation of dust and debris (e.g. by the fitting of cowls to electric motors). Shaft seals are incorporated in most stirrers and agitators and they will be subject to wear. This could result in product contamination, and therefore they should be inspected regularly as part of planned maintenance.

3.3.3 Post-process can handling equipment

Although the design of can-handling equipment might not be viewed strictly as a hygiene issue, incorrect design could result in post-process contamination with micro-organisms. As stated earlier, cans that have been thermally processed need to be cooled fairly rapidly to avoid any unnecessary deterioration in product quality. However, it is important that no microbial contamination is allowed to occur. The two possible routes for this are through the lid seal of the can, and through the main body of the can, should it become damaged. The former may occur if cans are manually handled while still hot and wet (the metal of the lid and body of the can will have expanded and a complete seal may not yet have been formed), or if the seal itself is deformed in some way. It is important to realise that deformation of the lid may not be a permanent feature, and that temporary microleaks in the seal can occur. Therefore, movement of batches of cans requires suitable machinery, and this machinery and the general protocols involved must be 'gentle' enough to avoid any physical damage to the can, and the springing open of the double seam, even if only for a fraction of a second.

The first operation will be the unloading of the cans from the retort (e.g. by fork-lift truck) and this needs to be done in such a way that there is no damage to the cans. The number of pieces of equipment within the conveying line should be kept to a minimum, and they should be designed as a complete unit, rather than as individual pieces of equipment joined together. The cans need to be conveyed in a controlled manner, and a build-up of cans should be avoided. One way of effecting this is to have each section of the conveyor unit operating at a slightly higher speed than the previous section.

Damage to cans may occur either by can-to-can impact or by impact between the can and the conveying system itself. Can-to-can impact can be eliminated by transporting them on properly adjusted cable runways or conveyors, avoiding overloading of the runway, and avoiding too many corners, turntable or 'twists'. Abuse between the can and the conveyor usually occurs as the cans pass from one section of the conveyor to another, or change direction or height on the conveyor. Examples are drop-turning upright cans to a forward rolling position and guides at exits of can-singling turntables (i.e. where cans are 'ordered' into single file).

A detailed consideration on good handling of post-process cans can be found in Thorpe (1994) and Thorpe and Everton (1968).

4. HYGIENIC PRACTICES

With the factory built to a good standard and the equipment designed and installed to meet hygiene requirements, the final pieces of the jigsaw are to ensure that the personnel working in the area follow best hygiene practices, that incursion by pests is controlled, and that efficient and meaningful cleaning of floors, walls and all equipment is carried out.

4.1 Personnel hygiene

People can be a vector for both microbial and physical contamination of foods, and adequate training of those involved in food processing needs to be given, to make them aware of the many seemingly innocuous actions which might compromise food safety or quality. Because many of the requirements appear trivial (whereas in reality they may be highly significant), personnel training is a high priority of the food processing industry. Both UK and EU food hygiene regulations contain several requirements relating to personnel hygiene. In addition, industry codes of practice (such as IFST, 1998 and IEHO, 1991) strongly suggest the taking of further precautions. Some of the main points of personnel hygiene and the broad reasoning behind them, as they relate to food production areas, are summarised below. Guidance from the Department of Health (DoH, 1996) emphasises the point that personnel carrying a food-transmittable disease or with skin infections or open wounds must not work in a food processing area.

- Everyone working in a food processing area must maintain a high level of personal cleanliness; all clothing must be clean, easily washable and suitable for the purpose, and protective clothing must be worn where appropriate. Outdoor clothes should not be allowed into food production areas. Protective clothing should include hairnets and beard coverings. Hair itself and dandruff are foreign body hazards for food, and the scalp can be a source of micro-organisms. Care should be taken with cuffs, as there is a risk of these inadvertently and unknowingly contaminating food and food-contact surfaces.

♦ No-one carrying a food-transmittable disease, or with infected wounds, skin infections, sores or diarrhoea may work in a food processing area. Anyone suffering from such conditions, or suspecting that they are suffering, must report it to the appropriate person. Pre-employment checks on personnel should be carried out and the workforce should be actively encouraged to report any potentially hazardous illnesses.

♦ There must be an adequate number of washbasins with hot and cold running water and flush lavatories available, as well as materials for cleaning and drying hands. Hands should be kept clean at all times by washing thoroughly in hot water with liquid soap. They should also be efficiently dried. Hand washing should be performed before handling any food or equipment, and in between handling raw and cooked food, as well as after visiting the toilet, combing the hair, eating, smoking or blowing the nose, or handling waste food or refuse. As hands are most likely to be in direct contact with food or food-contact surfaces, they are the main route for transfer of micro-organisms from people to food. This area is discussed in more detail below.

♦ The wearing of wrist-watches and jewellery in 'open food' areas should not be allowed, with the exception of plain wedding rings and plain sleeper earrings. The hazard here is that small parts of such jewellery (such as gemstones) may fall off onto the food processing line. For similar reasons, loose items should not be carried in this area. Strong smelling perfumes should not be worn, as there is the danger that they may taint foods, especially those with a high fat content. Nail varnish is prone to chipping and is not desirable in food processing areas.

- The risks of contamination from the nose, mouth and ears should be minimised by the prohibition of eating or chewing, and blowing onto spectacles. Similarly, smoking must not be allowed: in addition to the microbial risks, both physical (ash) and chemical (smoke taint) contamination would be likely. Coughs and sneezes can carry droplet infection for a considerable distance, and staff should be made aware of this danger; those with bad colds should not handle open food.

Hand hygiene

Contamination of food via the hands of personnel may be by direct contact of the food with hands or indirectly through poor practice such as handling and contaminating equipment that is subsequently used for food preparation. Micro-organisms residing on the hands can be either resident or transitory. Resident organism levels vary over the hand and are highest on the fingertips and under the nails. They reside as microcolonies attached to skin scales and are able to resist moderate desiccation and the antibacterial properties of chemicals in the skin. Transient organisms are acquired from the environment; in the food industry they include those acquired from handling raw materials, processed foods, equipment, contaminated clothing and touching other parts of the body. They are generally readily removed by washing (Taylor, 2000). Rings and watches worn on the hands may also be a source of these transient organisms (in addition to be being a foreign body hazard), and so should not be worn.

The purpose of hand washing is to remove desquamated cells (those essentially detached from the skin), sweat, sebaceous secretions and transient bacteria as well as any adhered organic material. It is important to wash hands effectively - it is easy to miss important areas of the hand. In the procedure illustrated below (first described by Ayliffe *et al.*, 1978), each step consists of 5 strokes forwards and 5 backwards. Care must be taken not to get cuffs wet, as this can then act as a reservoir for contamination.

Good handwashing technique

A correct hand-washing regime is very important in maintaining adequate hygiene in food processing factories, especially in 'high-care' areas, such as chilled food production facilities. Hands should be wetted and soap used from a dispenser. All parts of the hands and wrists should be rubbed, as shown below, with each step consisting of 5 strokes forward and backward.

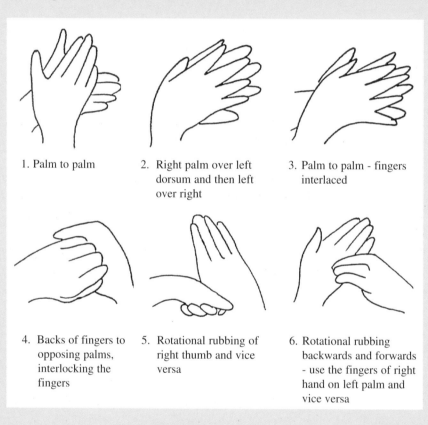

1. Palm to palm

2. Right palm over left dorsum and then left over right

3. Palm to palm - fingers interlaced

4. Backs of fingers to opposing palms, interlocking the fingers

5. Rotational rubbing of right thumb and vice versa

6. Rotational rubbing backwards and forwards - use the fingers of right hand on left palm and vice versa

References:

Ayliffe, G.A.J., Babb, J.R. and Quaraishi, A.H. (1978) A test of hygienic hand disinfection. Journal of Clinical Pathology, **31**: 923-928.

Taylor, J.H. and Holah, J.T. (2000) Hand hygiene in the food industry: a review. CCFRA Review No. 18.

The handwashing procedure described can be helped by keeping fingernails short and clean, and by the appropriate use of nail brushes. Providing that hands are cleaned of food or other debris, disinfectant wipes have been shown to be as effective as antibacterial soaps in removing micro-organisms from hands, especially when alcohol is incorporated (Taylor *et al.*, 2000). This means that good hand hygiene can be employed by personnel, even at times when it is difficult to leave the process line.

Drying of hands is an essential part of hand hygiene; damp or wet hands have the ability to transfer micro-organisms (i.e. the residents that are not removed by washing) onto other surfaces. Hot air drying for 45 seconds or two paper towels have been found to be generally effective.

With the necessity to wash hands frequently, the problem of occupational dermatitis will be encountered in some members of the workforce. Gloves can be worn to protect the hands, as well as, in some situations, protecting food from microbial contamination. However, wearing gloves results in the skin being occluded, giving rise to an increase in skin temperature, humidity, carbon dioxide concentration and acidity, which leads to an increase in the numbers of micro-organisms present. Thorough washing of hands needs to be carried out both before and after putting on gloves; they need to be changed every break and when they become damaged. The chemical constituents of the gloves need to be considered with respect to transferring plastic monomers or taints to foods

Footwear

Footwear has the potential to transfer physical and microbial contamination to floors over significant distances, especially when the floor is wet. Microbial transfer is also much greater when floors are wet. It is important that the systems employed for cleaning boots are properly used, as improper use can be both totally ineffective and, in some cases, result in water splashing on other clothing, thus compounding potential problems. Some specific issues to be considered with regard to footwear hygiene are given in the accompanying box.

Footwear hygiene

Various factors, sometimes conflicting, have to be considered when assessing the potential spread of contamination by footwear. For example, whilst the material and physical properties of the footwear should permit fast and effective cleaning in ways that will not encourage the spread of microbes (e.g. in droplets), they also have to offer slip resistance to help assure worker safety.

Whilst it has long been recognised that footwear can transfer contamination from one area to another, the extent and significance of this has not been clearly understood. A recent research project undertaken at CCFRA (Taylor *et al.*, 2000) led to a set of recommendations to help reconcile these seemingly conflicting requirements (see accompanying flow chart). Examples of the recommendations are:

- Minimise surplus water

- Use an appropriate footwear cleaning system (see decision tree)

- Boot baths are not recommended for high risk areas as they have limited effectiveness in removing organic soil

- Bootwashers can be very effective at removing gross organic soil and, by helping to minimise slip hazards, can contribute to worker safety. However, as they can also create and disperse water droplets, their use in high risk areas should be assessed in relation to the circumstances of use.

- Captive boots (i.e. those which remain within a processing area - either high or low risk) are appropriate for high-risk areas when used with an appropriate footwear cleaning system capable of microbial decontamination. Manual cleaning and washing machines, located in high risk areas, are best as they allow drying of the boots before use in production areas. An atomiser system with an alcohol-based disinfectant can be effective where there is little soil present.

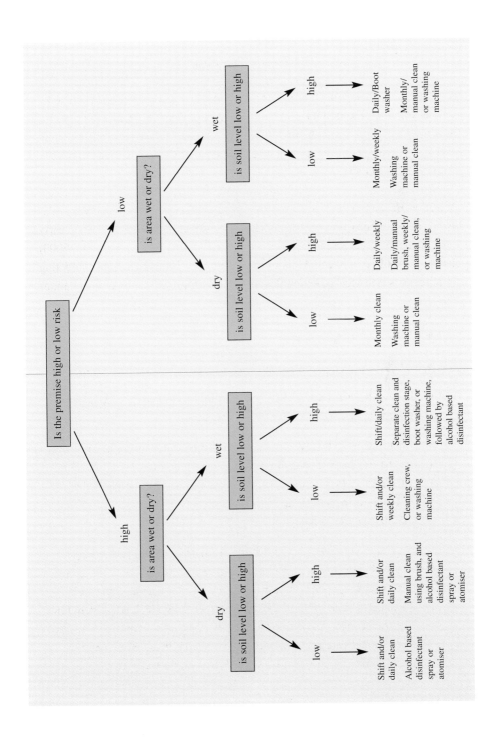

Is the premise high or low risk

high

is area wet or dry?

dry

is soil level low or high

low
Shift and/or
daily clean

Alcohol based
disinfectant
spray or
atomiser

high
Shift and/or
daily clean

Manual clean
using brush, and
alcohol based
disinfectant
spray or
atomiser

wet

is soil level low or high

low
Shift and/or
weekly clean

Cleaning crew,
or washing
machine

high
Shift/daily clean

Separate clean and
disinfection stage,
boot washer, or
washing machine,
followed by
alcohol based
disinfectant

low

is area wet or dry?

dry

is soil level low or high

low
Monthly clean

Washing
machine or
manual clean

high
Daily/weekly

Daily/manual
brush, weekly,
manual clean,
or washing
machine

wet

is soil level low or high

low
Monthly/weekly

Washing
machine or
manual clean

high
Daily/Boot
washer

Monthly/
manual clean
or washing
machine

4.2 Pest control

It is important to prevent pests from entering the production area wherever possible, and to have effective mechanisms for dealing with any that gain access. Rodents, birds and insects all carry the threat of microbial contamination to food, insects can easily become foreign bodies in products (if adequate precautions are not taken), and rodents could even end up eating the product!

The danger from flies

Flies can contaminate food in various ways:

- They regurgitate enzymes and other contents from their intestinal tract, in order to 'dissolve' the food they need to survive.

- They carry bacteria on their legs, body and hairs; these bacteria may subsequently grow on the food and result in spoilage of the food or present a safety problem.

- They lay eggs which, if left for a sufficient amount of time, develop into larvae and pupae.

They can be controlled in various ways, but these must be compatible with food safety. Control measures include:

- fly screens

- self-closing doors

- electronic fly killers

- chemical control (e.g. insecticides and attractants)

There are several stages to maintaining a pest-free production area:

- Keep the factory area clear of debris, especially waste food and packaging, so that pests are not attracted into the building

- Identify all openings in the roof, eaves and walls and either close or screen them off. Also, protect doors and windows with air curtains, strip curtains, netting or similar barriers

- If necessary, use rodent bait to control external pests. This should be carried out by trained personnel, possibly a specialist contractor, and due regard must be given to existing environmental legislation and regulations and codes of practices pertaining to wildlife (such as the UK Wildlife and Countryside Act and specific legislation made under it). Care must also be taken to prevent contamination of the food production area with any pest control substances.

- Leave space between walls and equipment or stored product, to allow adequate cleaning and inspection for any pests that may have gained access

- Insect 'knock-down' devices (Insectocutors) should be employed, except where there is a risk of dust explosions. These are best placed in areas of low light intensity for maximum effect, but should be kept away from processing lines, open food, filling machines, storage tanks and so on. They should also be sited away from doors and other openings, as they act by attracting insects towards them. Suitable trays to catch electrocuted insects should be used.

5. CLEANING AND DISINFECTION

However hygienically designed the premises and equipment are, and even if the best personnel hygiene standards are employed, it is inevitable that all food processing areas and machinery will accumulate dirt, debris and associated micro-organisms on a regular basis. The food materials being processed are likely to be the major source of contamination. It is undesirable to have 'old' food with its associated micro-organisms incorporated into product. Therefore, regular, structured cleaning and disinfection regimes have to be employed. Most of these will involve water-based detergents and disinfectants, but it is important to note that in dry food production areas the introduction of water is highly undesirable, and appropriate dry cleaning methods should be employed.

A complete sanitation programme involves the use of detergents to remove soil and debris and most micro-organisms, disinfectants to kill off any remaining micro-organisms, and potable water to remove the detergents and disinfectants (Holah, 2000a). It is important to note that there are two specific chemical functions: detergents (and usually water) for cleaning off debris, and disinfectants for removing and killing micro-organisms. There are also many ways in which these chemicals can be applied to the surfaces being cleaned. The exact protocols employed in a sanitation programme will depend on the nature of the debris that has to be removed, the degree of processing it might have undergone (that subjected to heat processing might be 'baked on' and be more difficult to remove), and the overall risk to the food being produced. Thus, more stringent measures might be taken in a 'high-care', chilled food production area, than in one preparing ingredients that are going to be heat processed in another part of the factory.

The sanitation programme addresses four key stages:

◆ The cleaning solution wetting the soil and the surface being cleaned
◆ The cleaning solution reacting with the soil components and the surface to facilitate their removal
◆ The prevention of recontamination of the cleaned surface with the soil
◆ The wetting of residual micro-organisms by disinfectant solutions and their removal from the surface

In practical terms, these four stages each involve the use of one or more of four major factors:

◆ Mechanical energy (e.g. scrubbing or spraying)
◆ Chemical energy (the nature of the detergent or disinfectant)
◆ Thermal energy (e.g. hot water or steam with cleaning agents)
◆ Time

Not all areas will need to be cleaned in the same way or at the same frequency. It is important to specify what gets cleaned, when and how cleaning takes place, who is responsible, the chemicals, materials and procedures to be used, and the precautions that need to be taken.

5.1 Cleaning chemicals (detergents)

The nature of the cleaning chemicals used will depend on both the nature of the surface to be cleaned and the type of soil or debris with which it is likely to be contaminated. For the majority of food processing operations it is usually possible to use one chemical cleaner only, although more specialised chemicals may be needed in some situations (e.g. ovens and CIP regimes). Many cleaning chemicals not only remove soil and debris, but are also quite efficient at removing attached micro-organisms, and when choosing chemicals for their cleaning ability, it is worth also considering this additional capability. Detergents can be assessed in terms of their surfactancy (wetting power), dispersion (breaking soil into smaller pieces) and suspension (preventing redeposition of the soil).

Water

Water is the basic ingredient of all 'wet' cleaning systems. It not only acts as a transport mechanism for the dissolved detergents, it is also capable of dissolving ionic compounds such as salt and sugars and for emulsifying fats if used at temperatures above the melting point of the fat. In high-pressure systems it also acts as an abrasive agent. However, it is generally not good at dissolving non-ionic compounds (e.g. oils and fats) and other chemicals need to be added for this purpose.

Organic surfactants

Organic surfactants are amphipolar - that is, they are made up of water-soluble and fat-soluble sections. They consist of a long non-polar (lipophilic or fat-soluble) chain and a polar (hydrophilic or water-soluble) head. The polar section can be either anionic, cationic or non-ionic (although cationic surfactants are less common). Amphipolar molecules act by reducing surface tension and by emulsifying the fats. In the surface tension-reducing effect, the polar part of the molecule disrupts the hydrogen bonding in water, causing the spherical droplets to collapse, which results in wetting of the surface. This allows the water to penetrate further into the soil and also into any irregularities in the surface being cleaned. The overall effect is an improvement in cleaning capabilities of the water. At the same time fat emulsification takes place; the hydrophobic part of the amphipolar molecule dissolves in any lipids present in the soil, while the hydrophilic part dissolves in water. This also facilitates the removal of the fat from the surface to which it is attached (Holah, 2000a).

Alkalis

Alkalis are often used as cleaning agents. They have several functions. As well as having bactericidal properties, strong alkalis such as caustic soda are efficient at hydrolysing proteins (the bonds between the individual amino acids in the protein chain are broken down, allowing the material to be solubilised and removed from surfaces). They are also efficient fat saponifiers - effectively converting a hydrophobic fat molecule into an amphipolar soap, which can be more easily removed. One of the main drawbacks with using alkaline detergents is their corrosive nature and the associated risk to those doing the cleaning. Weak alkalis can be used, but while being much less hazardous they are also less effective. Alkalis are also difficult to rinse off and form scums with soaps.

Chelating agents

Hard water ions (calcium and magnesium) can be a problem in some areas because, if present at high enough levels, they can restrict the effectiveness of surfactants - therefore, sequestering (chelating) agents are added to the solution to effectively remove them. They do this by forming soluble complexes with the ions, preventing them from precipitating. Ethylene diamine tetraacetic acid (EDTA) and some polyphosphates are the main chelating agents available. The latter are less expensive than EDTA, but do have drawbacks from an environmental pollution point of view. Alternatively, acid detergents can be used periodically to facilitate mineral soil removal.

5.2 Disinfectants

Although the detergent cleaning materials frequently remove a significant proportion of the microbial contamination present, an additional disinfection procedure is usually necessary to reduce further the viable microbial load present. This will be either by physically removing them (i.e. washing them away), or by killing them *in situ*, or both. Heat (i.e. using hot water or steam) is a very effective way of achieving this, but in most situations it is either technically or economically not feasible. For this reason, biocidal chemicals are usually used. Although there is a wide variety of chemicals that are biocidally effective, the range available for use in the cleaning of food processing areas is more limited. Many effective compounds, such as phenolics, are prone to tainting food and are unsuitable for use. Others are ruled out because of safety issues. In all cases, it is necessary to have removed all heavy soiling and gross debris before applying the disinfectants, as they are readily inactivated by organic material (Thorpe, 1989).

The most commonly used disinfectants are:

- chlorine-releasing compounds
- quaternary ammonium compounds
- amphoterics
- quaternary ammonium/amphoteric mixtures

Chlorine-releasing compounds are the most widely used disinfectants in the UK. The most common are hypochlorite and the slow-releasing chloramines and dichlorodimethylhydantoin. These have a wide range of activity, including some effect against spores, and are relatively inexpensive. However, they are readily inactivated by organic matter, and potentially can have an adverse effect on the environment.

Quaternary ammonium compounds are amphipolar, cationic detergents that are derived from substituted ammonium salts with a chlorine or bromine atom. Although having little effect on spores, they are both relatively environmentally and operative friendly.

Amphoterics are based on the amino acid glycine, and are characterised by having both a positive and negative charge on the molecule. They share similar activities and benefits with the quaternary ammonium compounds.

In addition to these compounds, peracetic acid is an effective disinfectant, particularly against spores, but it is a hazardous chemical to use, being a very strong oxidising agent. Also, ethanol and isopropyl alcohol wipes and sprays are often employed in situations where the use of large volumes of water is not possible.

Novel methods of disinfection

Two potential novel technologies for reducing microbial contamination in food processing factories, from a hygiene point of view, are ozone and high intensity pulsed light. Although very different from each other, they both have the advantage of leaving no chemical residues; thus, production can recommence almost immediately after use, and the risk of subsequent chemical contamination or tainting is eliminated.

Initial research with ozone has been quite promising: it was effective at killing both micro-organisms attached to surfaces and those contained in an aerosol, to approximately the same degree. Additional potential advantages over chemical disinfectants include its ability to penetrate areas inaccessible to chemical fogs; reduced storage problems (it could be produced when required); and flexibility (it could be used to deodorise vehicles and storage areas).

In contrast, although the hypothetical mode of action of high intensity pulsed light indicates promise, preliminary work with small-scale apparatus has failed to produce any consistently useful effects. Work in this area continues to optimise the technique.

References:

Taylor, J. and Chana, D. (2000). The evaluation of ozone for airborne and surface disinfection. R&D Report 109. Campden & Chorleywood Food Research Association

Earnshaw, R.G. (1996). Non-thermal methods; realisation of technology. Proceedings of 1996 EFFoST symposium: Minimal processing of foods

5.3 Application of detergents and disinfectants

The items that may need to be regularly cleaned in food processing areas include walls, floors, processing machinery (e.g. slicers, mixers, extruders), and other product contact and non-contact surfaces (e.g. tables, conveyor belts, pipes). How often these need to be cleaned will depend entirely on the type of food being processed, how it is processed and the degree of risk and hazard likely to be associated with the build up of debris and associated micro-organisms in the processing area. The methods employed to apply the chemicals will depend on what is being cleaned and the associated problems, such as cross-contamination.

For small areas, simple hand tools such as brushes and cloths can be used. However, for larger areas, specialist mechanical equipment may be required to apply the chemicals and also the required mechanical energy. Chemicals may be applied as low-pressure mists, foams or gels, whilst mechanical energy is provided by high- or low-pressure water jets, or powered scrubbing brushes. If chemicals are being applied manually, the concentration and temperature of the chemicals used may be limited, for reasons of operator safety. This will usually mean that the time taken to do the job will increase, and it may be more economical to use mechanical equipment. However, in some situations (e.g. cleaning while processing operations are on-going), some mechanical solutions may not be acceptable: high-pressure hoses may generate too much mist or spray, which may result in contamination of the processing line. Brief descriptions of some of the application methods are given below.

Mists, foams and gels

These are all methods by which detergents and disinfectants can be applied to surfaces in order to prolong the contact time.

♦ Foams work on the basis of forming a layer of bubbles above the surface to be cleaned (by the incorporation of air into the cleaning fluid); these then collapse, so bathing the surface in fresh detergent or disinfectant. The key element is for the bubbles to collapse at the optimum rate, so that fresh cleaning agent is continually applied, but ensuring that contact time is long enough for it to have an effect.

♦ Gels are thixotropic cleaning chemicals which are fluid at high and low concentrations, but become thick and gelatinous at concentrations of approximately 5-10%. They are easy to apply through various high- and low-pressure systems, and physically adhere to the surface.

♦ Misting will only 'wet' vertical smooth surfaces, and contact times are usually 5 minutes or less. Mists also, by their nature, form aerosols, which can be a health hazard, so that only weak solutions of cleaning agents can be used. However, misting is very useful on cleaned surfaces for applying disinfectants, and is the most usual form of such application.

Fogging systems

Fogging systems are used to create and disperse a disinfectant aerosol to reduce airborne micro-organism levels, and also to apply disinfectant to areas that are difficult to reach, such as overhead surfaces. Fogging is most effective using compressed air-driven fogging nozzles producing particles of about 10-20 microns in diameter. It is only effective for surface disinfection if sufficient chemical can be deposited onto the surface, and it is unlikely that this will occur on vertical (e.g. walls) and underside (e.g. ceilings) surfaces. As it involves the formation of aerosols, it does pose inhalation risks, and sufficient time (usually 45-60 minutes) has to be allowed before the workforce can re-enter the production area.

Fogging disinfection research

Research by CCFRA and Silsoe Research Institute has looked at the factors that relate to the rate of dispersal and deposition of disinfectant fogs. Gravity and inertia were found to be important factors in the movement of the fog. Movement also depended on droplet size, which has implications for users of fogging systems. Particles of 25 microns fell out near the nozzle and did not reach the far side of the room being disinfected. However, particles of 2.5 micron size, although reaching all areas of the room, remained airborne for a long period of time, potentially causing safety problems for operators entering the room after fogging. As expected, the greatest reduction of microbial contamination occurred close to the floor.

Reference:

MAFF (1998) A practical guide to the disinfection of food processing factories and equipment using fogging. Based on the results of a project funded by MAFF and industry through the LINK Advanced and Hygienic Manufacturing Programme.

Cleaning in-place

Floors, walls and major food contact and non-contact surfaces such as conveyor belts and tables can be cleaned *in situ*. Where feasible, equipment should be dismantled for effective and complete cleaning. However, in some situations, such as closed systems of pipework and associated vessels and equipment, this is not practical, and the preferred technique of cleaning in-place (CIP) without dismantling is used. This is now widely established; in many installations, due to their size and complexity, it is impossible to do otherwise (Timperley, 1997).

In CIP, higher chemical and thermal energy inputs can be used than in manual cleaning - i.e. stronger chemicals and higher temperatures. The mechanical or kinetic energy is provided by turbulent flow in pipelines and the impingement of jets in vessels.

The design of equipment that is going to be cleaned in-place is especially important. It must be free from crevices and made of material that is able to withstand prolonged contact with detergents, acids and disinfectants at the cleaning temperatures used. The finish of the product contact surfaces has an effect on cleaning times, especially if the product residues are tenacious. All equipment needs to be self-draining, and horizontal runs of pipework should have a fall of about 1 in 100 to drain to the lowest points in the system. Dead-legs, often formed by blanked-off tee pieces, are a particular problem, as the cleaning fluid will not be able to gain effective access to them, and all kinetic energy input will be lost. In addition, any detergent or disinfectant that does gain access will be difficult to flush out before food production runs are restarted, potentially leading to chemical contamination and taint problems.

When and how to clean

As well as determining which chemicals are applied in cleaning regimes, and their method of application, cleaning and disinfection procedures are concerned with when the programme is implemented and the sequence in which equipment and environmental surfaces are cleaned. They also take note of safety and environmental issues - so that water (the principal cleaning chemical) is used efficiently, and chemicals are used at their optimum conditions.

Production staff should be encouraged to consider the implications of production practices on subsequent cleaning and disinfection programmes, for example by cleaning up large product spillages during production. During a scheduled cleaning programme, the sequence in which cleaning activities are undertaken should ensure that, once a product contact surface has been disinfected, it is not subsequently recontaminated during the procedure. This effectively means cleaning at a 'room' level, such that all environmental surfaces and equipment in the area are cleaned at the same time, rather than on a line-by-line basis, which merely spreads contamination around the room. The sequence recommended by Holah (2000a) is as follows:

- Remove gross soil from production equipment
- Remove gross soil from environmental surfaces
- Rinse down environmental surfaces (to at least 2m in height for walls)
- Rinse down equipment and flush to drain
- Clean environment surfaces, usually in the order of drains, walls and floors
- Rinse environmental surfaces
- Clean equipment
- Rinse equipment
- Disinfect equipment and rinse if required
- Fog (if required)

The frequency with which areas are cleaned will largely depend on the type of processing area and the nature of run times (e.g. is the production line run on a continuous shift system, and is there a weekend shutdown?). Ideally, production should not occur in the area being cleaned, but in exceptional circumstances, where this is not possible, other lines or areas should be screened off to prevent transfer of debris and other contaminants by the cleaning process.

Periodically (e.g. weekly or monthly) procedures should be undertaken to thoroughly clean equipment to a level beyond that undertaken, say, on a daily basis. This normally involves additional equipment dismantling and/or the application of increased cleaning energy. Periodic practices also include the more infrequent tasks of cleaning ceilings and overhead fittings (Holah, 2000b).

It is important to keep equipment used for cleaning and disinfecting high-care areas separate from that used for low-care areas.

6. HYGIENE MONITORING

It is important to know whether the cleaning and disinfection regimes undertaken are resulting in the required cleanliness, both in terms of removal of soil and debris, and in the destruction of micro-organisms. Routine hygiene testing comprises the day-to-day monitoring and verification necessary to check that processes designed to reduce microbiological numbers and levels of debris, such as those identified in a HACCP plan, are effective.

The first step in assessing the effectiveness of a cleaning programme is through a simple visual inspection: is there any evidence for gross debris remaining? are surfaces greasy? or is there evidence of the remains of cleaning residues (that might subsequently result in chemical contamination of food)? Even if surfaces look clean, micro-organisms may remain. Extensive details of when and how to take samples from the food processing environment (including sampling and swabbing techniques, general microbiological methods, and how to assure statistical validity of results) are given in Holah (1999), and some of the biochemical and molecular methods used are described in Jones (2000).

How to sample

Specific microbiological sampling is typically for the total number of viable micro-organisms (the Total Viable Count or TVC) as a measurement of the ability of a range of micro-organisms to survive or grow through a particular cleaning operation. However, monitoring for both debris and micro-organisms in combination is the most widely used method for monitoring hygiene status, as the techniques employed are rapid and can give virtually on-the-spot indications of the situation, allowing real-time control to determine whether cleaning needs to be repeated before production is restarted. Predominantly these are based on the detection of adenosine triphosphate (ATP), although recently commercial techniques based on the detection of proteins have been developed. ATP is present in all living organisms (it is the primary energy transfer unit for all metabolic processes), and in large quantities in a variety of food products. As food debris is likely to be the major type of debris on a process line, ATP analysis is a very good indicator of the overall cleanliness of the area being sampled (see Box).

When to sample

Sampling can be undertaken before, during and after production, depending on its purpose. Whereas for verifying that a cleaning programme is effective, sampling is generally taken after production (and after cleaning), monitoring the performance of a bootwasher, for example, by sampling the floor, may be taken during production. In monitoring the effect of an operation, it is also important to have data for microbial and debris levels before that operation (e.g. before and after production, but before the cleaning regime). However, results have to be treated in context. A processing line with an input of raw poultry is likely to have a very high microbiological load before cleaning. It is also important to compare results from sampling over a period of time, to indicate any trends. It may be that a clean-down at a certain time of day or year is less effective than at other times. Even if the end result is deemed satisfactory, it may highlight a factor that should be addressed to prevent it from becoming a problem.

What to sample

This very much depends on what activity is being monitored. To monitor the effectiveness of general cleaning regimes, it is necessary to sample walls, floors, the processing line and specific pieces of equipment. For example, a misting disinfection technique may result in effective sanitation of horizontal surfaces, but be inefficient at cleaning vertical surfaces. Specific sampling of equipment should fit in with what the HACCP analysis has indicated are the critical points with reference to final product quality and safety. For example, the cleaning of meat slicing machines in high-risk areas is often critical to limit the microbial contamination of the product, and will therefore need to be monitored. It is more useful to sample the points on the machine that directly contact the product, and those that are most difficult to clean - for example, the shear edge, the 'gripper box' or the meat feed conveyor, rather than flat surfaces on the exterior of the machine.

ATP analysis

ATP (adenosine triphosphate) is found in all living organisms and in food. Its detection can, therefore, be used as a means of monitoring the hygiene status of food contact surfaces and processing equipment. ATP can be analysed in a bioluminescent reaction, utilising the firefly enzyme luciferase, and its substrate luciferin. In the reaction, luciferin is oxidised by the enzyme to oxyluciferin; this oxidation uses up one molecule of ATP per molecule of luciferin and produces one photon of light. The amount of light produced can be measured in a luminometer, in Relative Light Units (RLU), and it is a relatively straightforward task to relate this to the amount of ATP present in the sample.

In two industrial cleaning trials, the effectiveness of the cleaning regime was assessed by comparing the ATP levels on the surface before and after cleaning. Test samples (swabs) were allocated to RLU groups - the lower the group number then the lower the ATP level and the cleaner the surface. Preliminary comparisons with conventional microbiological analyses can help establish a cut-off point at which surfaces might be deemed to have been cleaned sufficiently - say RLU group 2 or below.

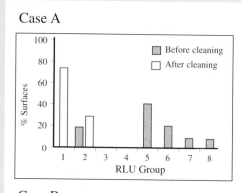

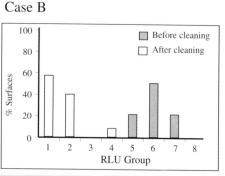

In Case A, the pre-cleaning samples fell into the higher RLU groups, while the post-cleaning samples fell into the lower groups, demonstrating that cleaning was effective at all sites sampled. In contrast, in Case B, even after cleaning, some surface samples fell into RLU group 4, and so would require re-cleaning under the above criteria.

Holah, J., Gibson, H and Hawronskyj, J.M. (1995) The use of ATP bioluminescence to monitor surface hygiene. European Food and Drink Review, Autumn 1995, 82-88

Jones, J.L. (2000). Molecular methods in food analysis: principles and examples. Key Topics in Food Science and Technology No. 1. Campden & Chorleywood Food Research Association

Obviously, if a particular problem has been identified, then extra specific sampling may be carried out, to identify both the nature of the problem and its source. Highly sophisticated analytical techniques and equipment are now available to assist in this; ribotyping, a type of genetic fingerprinting, is one such technique. This involves the automatic analysis of the DNA coding for the ribosomal RNA of a micro-organism at the molecular level, to yield a genetic fingerprint. This allows not only the species of organism to be identified, but also the specific isolate (see Jones, 2000 for a fuller description of molecular methods in food analysis).

Relating product contamination with failures in cleaning regime

During routine testing at CCFRA, a *Listeria* species was isolated from a ham sandwich. This was identified as a specific strain of *L.monocytogenes* and samples were taken from processing equipment and the surrounding environment as well as from raw materials and personnel working in the production area. Matching 'fingerprints' were found on staff shoes, the floor of a particular area of the processing hall, and the handle of a piece of equipment, but not in any area before this in the processing chain. As a result, the source of the contamination was quickly pinpointed, and cleaning procedures were modified to eliminate the problem, without, in this instance, the need for a product recall.

Reference:

Broomfield, P.L.E. (1996) Molecular typing of bacterial isolates as a contract service. Microbiology Europe 4(4): 24-26.

7. CONCLUSIONS

Hygiene issues for the food manufacturing industry go far beyond the ultimate, but simplistic, aspects of prevention of contamination with dirt and micro-organisms. As well as also encompassing issues such as the prevention of physical and chemical contamination, they need to address the fundamental aspects that make this prevention of contamination possible. In broad terms, the areas that need to be addressed are:

♦ Suitable geographical location of factory
♦ Correct design of factory - externally (to protect the product from contamination) and internally (to maintain product segregation, maximise product flow, and optimise air-flow and personnel movements)
♦ Appropriate use of construction materials, both internal and external, to reduce the build-up of debris and micro-organisms and facilitate cleaning
♦ Correct design of equipment, so that it can be adequately cleaned, and to ensure that the risk of physical contamination (e.g. metal shards, nuts and bolts) is minimised
♦ Correct lay-out of equipment, to facilitate optimum movement of product and personnel
♦ Ensuring that personnel maintain hygienic practices
♦ Use of appropriate detergents and disinfectants, at the right time, and in the right way, ensuring that the cleaning programme does not cause, rather than prevent, contamination
♦ Identifying and implementing appropriate systems for monitoring hygienic practices and the effectiveness of cleaning systems

As emphasised in the opening sections of this book, hygiene in its broadest sense involves all measures taken to prevent contamination of food with any contaminant - and this might be microbiological, chemical or physical. The principles and examples described through the book should illustrate that good hygienic practice is as much about the philosophy of the approach as the mechanics of the methods used. Both are equally important and both, when used appropriately, provide tools with which to implement a broader HACCP-based safety assurance system.

8. REFERENCES AND FURTHER READING

Anon (1993). Council Directive 93/43/EEC of 14 June 1993 on the hygiene of foodstuffs. Official Journal of the EC L175, 19 July 1993, p1.

Anon (1998). Directive 98/37/EC of the European parliament and of the Council of 22 June 1998 on the approximation of the laws of the Member States relating to machinery. Official Journal of the EC L207, 23 July 1998, p1.

Ayliffe, G.A.J., Babb, J.R. and Quaraishi, A.H. (1978). A test of hygienic hand disinfection. Journal of Clinical Pathology, 31: 923-928

Broomfield, P.L.E. (1996). Molecular typing of bacterial isolates as a contract service. Microbiology Europe 4(4): 24-26

Brown, K.L. (1996). Guidelines on air quality standards for the food industry. Guideline No. 12. Campden & Chorleywood Food Research Association

Brown, K. L. and Hall, K.E. (1999). The relationship between risk of product contamination and airborne microbial challenge - a preliminary study. R&D Report 83. Campden & Chorleywood Food Research Association.

Burfoot, D., Reawell, S., Brown, K., Duke, N., Newton, K., Morgan, W. and Sainter, J. (2001). Best practice guidelines on air flows in high-care and high risk areas. Silsoe Research Institute.

Campbell, A.J. (1995). Guidelines for the prevention and control of foreign bodies in food. Guideline No. 5. Campden & Chorleywood Food Research Association.

CFDRA (1982). The principles of design for hygienic food processing machinery. Technical memorandum No. 289. Campden & Chorleywood Food Research Association.

CFDRA (1983). Hygienic design of food processing equipment. Technical Manual No. 7. Campden & Chorleywood Food Research Association.

Dawson, D. (1998). Water quality for the food industry: an introductory manual. Campden & Chorleywood Food Research Association.

Dawson, D. (2000). Water quality for the food industry: management and microbiological issues. Campden & Chorleywood Food Research Association.

Department of Health (1994). Guidelines for the safe production of heat-preserved foods.

Department of Health (1996). Food Handlers. Fitness to work. Guidelines for Food Business Managers. Prepared by an Expert Working Group convened by the Department of Health.

Earnshaw, R.G. (1996). Non-thermal methods; realisation of technology. Proceedings of 1996 EFFoST symposium: Minimal processing of foods.

Guzewich, J. and Ross, P. (1999). Evaluation of risks related to microbiological contamination of ready-to-eat food by food preparation workers and the effectiveness of interventions to minimse those risks. Food and Drug Administration White Paper.

Holah, J.T. (1997). Microbiological control of food industry process waters. Guidelines on the use of chlorine dioxide and bromine as alternatives to chlorine. Guideline 15. Campden & Chorleywood Food Research Association

Holah, J.T. (1999). Effective microbiological sampling of food processing environments. Guideline No. 20. Campden & Chorleywood Food Research Association

Holah, J.T. (2000a). Cleaning and disinfection. In: Chilled Foods: A Comprehensive Guide. (Eds. M.F. Stringer and C. Dennis). Woodhead Publishing

Holah, J.T. (2000b). Food processing equipment design and cleanability.. Flair-Flow Europe Technical Manual F-FE 377A/00

Holah, J., Gibson, H and Hawronskyj, J.M. (1995). The use of ATP bioluminescence to monitor surface hygiene. European Food and Drink Review, Autumn 1995, 82-88

Holah, J.T., Hall, K.E., Holder, J. Rogers, S.J., Taylor, J,H, and Brown, K.L. (1995). Airborne micro-organism levels in food processing environments. R&D Report 12. Campden & Chorleywood Food Research Association

Holah, J. and Thorpe, R. (2000). The hygienic design of chilled foods plant. pp355-396 in Chilled Foods: a comprehensive guide (Eds. M. Stringer and C. Dennis).

IEHO (1991). The Food Hygiene Handbook. Institution of Environmental Health Officers

IFST (1998). Food and Drink. Good Manufacturing Practice. A guide to its responsible management. 4th edition. Institute of Food Science and Technology.

Jones, J.L. (2000). Molecular methods in food analysis: principles and examples. Key Topics in Food Science and Technology No. 1. Campden & Chorleywood Food Research Association

Jowett, R. (1980). Hygienic Design and Operation of Food Plant. Society of Chemical Industry/Ellis Horwood.

Leaper, S. (1997). HACCP: A practical guide. Technical Manual No. 38. 2nd Edition. Campden & Chorleywood Food Research Association

MAFF (1998). A practical guide to the disinfection of food processing factories and equipment using fogging. Based on the results of a project funded by MAFF and industry through the LINK Advanced and Hygienic Manufacturing Programme.

Mortimore, S. and Wallace, C. (1998). HACCP: A practical approach. Aspen Publishers

Seymour, I.J. (1999). Review of current industry practice on fruit and vegetable decontamination. Review No. 14. Campden & Chorleywood Food Research Association.

Taylor, J.H. (2000). Hand hygiene in the food industry. Review No. 18. Campden & Chorleywood Food Research Association.

Taylor, J. and Chana, D. (2000). The evaluation of ozone for airborne and surface disinfection. R&D Report 109. Campden & Chorleywood Food Research Association

Taylor, J.H. and Holah, J.T. (2000). Hand hygiene in the food industry: a review. Review 18 Campden & Chorleywood Food Research Association.

Taylor, J.H., Kaur, M. and Walker, H. (2000). Hand and footwear hygiene: an investigation to define best practice. R&D Report No. 110. Campden & Chorleywood Food Research Association.

Thorpe, R.H. (1989). Hygiene and sanitation. European food and Drink Review. Summer: 57-60

Thorpe, R. (1994). Guidelines on the prevention of visible can defects. Technical Manual No. 37. Campden & Chorleywood Food Research Association.

Thorpe, R.H. and Everton, J.R. (1968). Post-process sanitation in canneries. Technical Manual No. 1 Campden & Chorleywood Food Research Association.

Timperley, D.A. (1993). Guidelines for the design and construction of floors for food production areas. Technical Manual No. 40. Campden & Chorleywood Food Research Association.

Timperley, D.A. and Timperley, A.W. (1993). Hygienic designs of meat slicing machines. Technical Memorandum No. 679. Campden & Chorleywood Food Research Association.

Timperley, A.W. (1994). Design and construction of walls, ceilings and services for food production areas. Technical Manual No. 44. Campden & Chorleywood Food Research Association.

Timperley, A.W. (1997). Hygienic design of liquid handling equipment for the food industry. Technical Manual 17. 2nd Edition. Campden & Chorleywood Food Research Association.